LOOK

I'm a Maths Wizard

DK

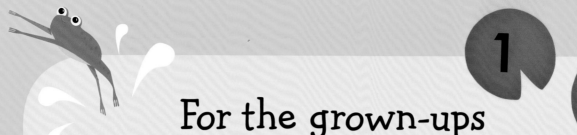

For the grown-ups

This book is full of hands-on activities that will tap straight into your child's natural mathematical curiosity. Each activity is designed to let your child play and learn with all their senses. Together, you can grow their love of maths, their creative problem-solving, and their understanding of the world.

Here are a few tips to help you along the way:

The lightbulb speech bubbles at the start of the activities suggest a learning objective for each game, but these should not limit your child's play. Involve your child in the preparation of each activity, let them follow the instructions, but also let them try out their own ideas and explore in ways that they find interesting. You never know what they might discover!

•

Your child should be supervised when experimenting with these activities, but try to give them time and space to lead the direction of play. The questions in this book are suggestions. Let your child ask, and answer, their own questions.

•

Adult Alert stars show where your child will need extra grown-up help.

•

Protect the area where your child will be playing and encourage them to wear old clothes. Be especially careful when using food colouring, which can mark fabrics and temporarily stain skin. Being prepared lets your child enjoy themselves to their fullest. Making a mess is part of the fun and learning!

Adult ALERT!

DK | Penguin Random House

Editor Hélène Hilton
Designer and Illustrator Charlotte Milner
Series Designer Rachael Parfitt-Hunt
Editorial Assistance Sally Beets, Clare Lloyd
Additional Design and Illustration Kitty Glavin, Rachael Hare, Victoria Palastanga
DTP Designer Mohammad Rizwan
Educational Consultant Penny Coltman
Photographer Lol Johnson
Jacket Designer Charlotte Milner
Jacket Coordinator Issy Walsh
Producer, Pre-Production Sophie Chatellier
Senior Producer Amy Knight
Managing Editor Penny Smith
Managing Art Editor Mabel Chan
Creative Director Helen Senior
Publishing Director Sarah Larter

First published in Great Britain in 2019 by
Dorling Kindersley Limited
80 Strand, London WC2R 0RL

Copyright © 2019 Dorling Kindersley Limited
A Penguin Random House Company
10 9 8 7 6 5 4 3 2 1
001–307831–Sept/2019

All rights reserved.
No part of this publication may be reproduced, stored in or introduced into a retrieval system, or transmitted, in any form, or by any means (electronic, mechanical, photocopying, recording, or otherwise), without the prior written permission of the copyright owner.

A CIP catalogue record for this book is available from the British Library.
ISBN: 978-0-2413-1587-3

Printed in China

The publisher would like to thank the following for their kind permission to reproduce their photographs:
(Key: a-above; b-below/bottom; c-centre; f-far; l-left; r-right; t-top)
27 Dreamstime.com: Xjjx (crb)
All other images © Dorling Kindersley
For further information see: www.dkimages.com

And a **big thank you** to Thomas Hellyar who acted as model and maths wizard.

A WORLD OF IDEAS:
SEE ALL THERE IS TO KNOW

www.dk.com

Contents

Little minds have big ideas!

You don't need a **fancy calculator,** or a whiteboard full of **big numbers** to be a maths wizard. You already have everything you need: **your brain** and **your amazing senses**!

Curious questions

Maths is full of puzzles to solve, things to work out, and brain teasers. Here are some questions to ask yourself as you play.

- How can maths ideas be useful in the real world?

- Where can I spot maths being used around me?

- How can I learn even more about these maths ideas and topics?

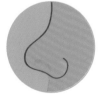

4

Your maths senses

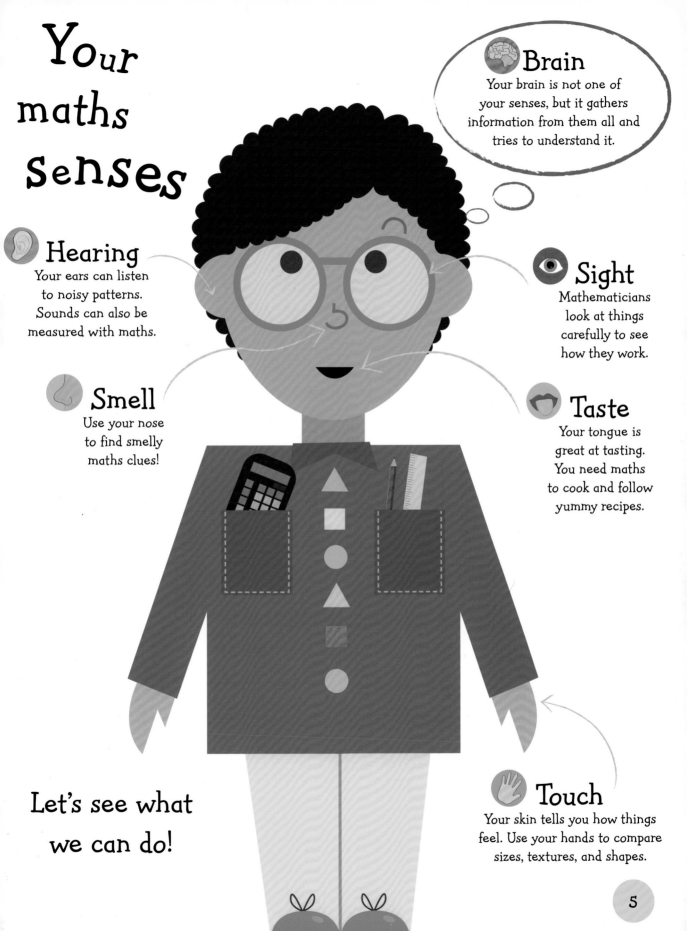

Brain
Your brain is not one of your senses, but it gathers information from them all and tries to understand it.

Hearing
Your ears can listen to noisy patterns. Sounds can also be measured with maths.

Smell
Use your nose to find smelly maths clues!

Sight
Mathematicians look at things carefully to see how they work.

Taste
Your tongue is great at tasting. You need maths to cook and follow yummy recipes.

Touch
Your skin tells you how things feel. Use your hands to compare sizes, textures, and shapes.

Let's see what we can do!

Maths treasure hunt

Maths is all around you! Ask your grown-up to take you on a **nature walk** to gather maths treasures.

Learn to find maths in your everyday life with this activity.

Can you count your maths treasures?

Wash your treasures (and your hands!) thoroughly. Things you pick up can be a bit germy.

What's maths?

Maths is all about **numbers**, **shapes**, **measurements**, and **patterns**. These things help us understand our world. You can use maths as a tool to solve problems and create solutions.

What shapes can you see?

Pebbles

Pinecone

Which of your treasures feels the lightest and which is the heaviest?

Feel and count the lines on your leaf.

Feather

Which treasures do you have most and fewest of?

Leaf

What colours can you spot on your nature walk?

Shells

Sorting sizes

From the **tiniest** pebble you picked up, to the **heaviest** rock, and the **longest** feather, sort your nature treasures **from the smallest to the biggest.**

Play this sorting game to learn about size. Use words such as big, small, bigger, smaller, biggest, and smallest.

1

Start with two pebbles. **Compare** them to see which is **bigger** and which is **smaller.**

Small stones on this side.

Big stones on this side.

2

Add another pebble, deciding if it is the smallest, biggest, or in the middle. Keep going until all your stones are sorted by size.

Play this game with toys if you haven't been on a treasure hunt yet.

Biggest

Smallest

How else can you sort your nature objects?

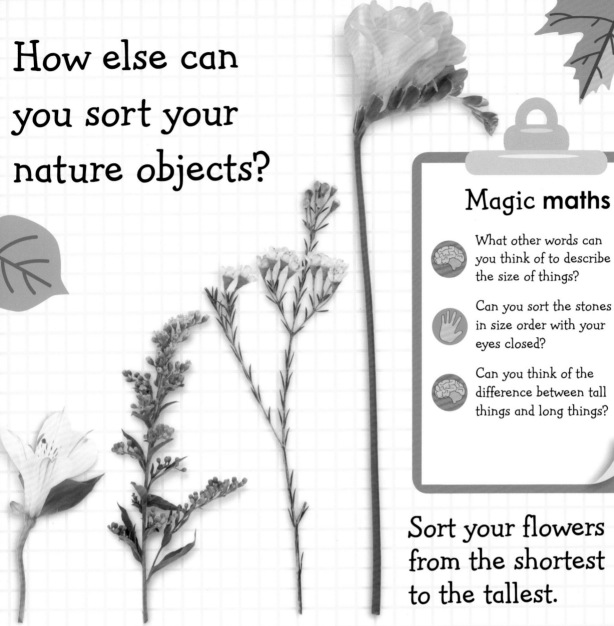

Magic **maths**

- What other words can you think of to describe the size of things?

- Can you sort the stones in size order with your eyes closed?

- Can you think of the difference between tall things and long things?

Sort your flowers from the shortest to the tallest.

Sort your sticks from shortest to longest.

There are lots of ways to sort your treasures. None of them is wrong if they follow a pattern.

Clever counting

Numbers are super useful to know. Learn your numbers to 10 and beyond with these awesome **mini games.** You'll soon be counting everything around you!

These games teach you how to count objects one by one and the order of numbers from 1 to 10.

Boing!

Frog hopscotch

Cut big leaf shapes out of green card and number them. Stick them to the floor with sticky tack to make sure you don't slip over. Hop from pad to pad like a little frog, counting as you go.

Count each pad as you hop like a little frog.

Start here

Adult ALERT!

You can make the hopscotch more challenging by going beyond 10, or by counting backwards.

You can add bubble wrap to the pads to make them squishy.

Your toys all wait to cross on the same side of the river.

Count each toy as you help it cross.

Cross the river

Make a paper river. Collect little toys and place them all on one side of the river. Count each toy as you help them cross the river one by one. How many toys are crossing?

Number fingers

Your fingers and thumbs are great tools to count to 10! Make these special gloves by sticking numbers on the fingers.

Adult ALERT!

Make the numbers with sticky labels or cut them out of felt and glue them on.

old gloves

Number bugs

Number bugs teach you to match a quantity with its written number.

Make these cute number bugs to practise your **counting** skills and to start **writing numbers.**

You will need:

pebbles

red and yellow paint

paintbrush

marker pen

big leaves

1 Choose **10 pebbles** to turn into number bugs. Paint the pebbles yellow and red.

2 Once the paint is dry, **add details** with a marker pen. Give each bug between 1 and 10 **spots or black stripes.**

Buzz!

Count the spots and black stripes on each bug to make sure you have all the numbers from 1 to 10.

Red pebbles are ladybirds.

Yellow pebbles are bees. Its face doesn't count as a stripe!

3

Choose ten leaves and **number them** from 1 to 10.

Play the **number** **bugs game** by **matching** each **bug** to its **leaf**.

Magic maths

How did your pebbles feel before you painted them?

Why do you think real bees and ladybirds have spots and stripes?

Can you practise writing your numbers in the air with a finger?

If you don't have pebbles or leaves, you can still play by making paper bugs and leaves.

13

Hungry adding robot

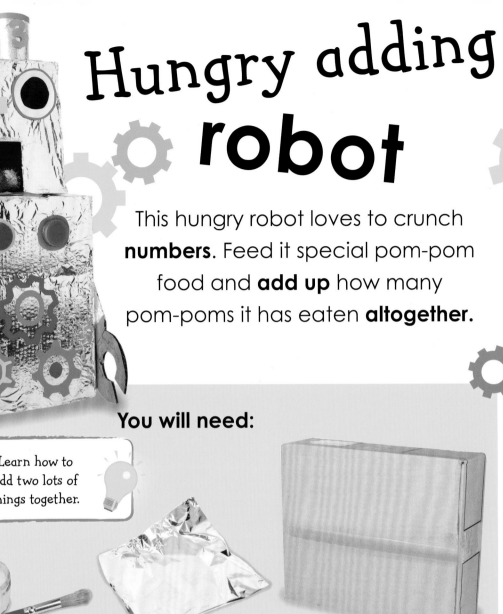

This hungry robot loves to crunch **numbers**. Feed it special pom-pom food and **add up** how many pom-poms it has eaten **altogether**.

You will need:

Learn how to add two lots of things together.

glue and brush

kitchen foil

cardboard box

scissors

2 cardboard tubes

coloured paper

sticky tack

pom-poms

1

Cover your box with **glue** and stick on **kitchen foil.**

Make me a square mouth flap.

2

Carefully **cut out** a **flap** in your box to make the robot's mouth.

Cut it!

Adult ALERT!

I'm hungry! Is my dinner coming soon?

Magic maths

- When do you add things together in your everyday life?

- Can you feel and count how many pom-poms the robot is eating?

- Try swapping the tubes around. What do you notice happens to the numbers of pom-poms?

Cut two holes in the top of the box for the tubes.

3

Cut **two circles** into the top of the box. Slot the **cardboard tubes** into the holes Cover them with **foil**.

2

sticky tack

4

Decorate the robot's face with eyes and a nose. Cut out **paper numbers** and fix them to each tube with sticky tack.

Make me a body with another foil-covered box.

Time for dinner!

Count the robot food pom-poms as you drop them in (match the number on the tube). **Find the total** by counting the pom-poms in its mouth **altogether**.

How many are there altogether?

Amazing **adding**

Adding means counting two or more groups of things **altogether**. You can write this as a number sentence. The **plus sign +** means add and the **equals sign =** means altogether.

plus sign · equals sign · altogether

2 + 3 = 5

17

Carnival cans

It's carnival time! How many cans will you knock down, and **how many will be left?**

Learn how subtraction (taking away) works and how to write it as a number sentence.

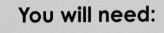

You will need:

10 cans

strips of colourful paper

pretty tape

For the ball:

rice

clingfilm

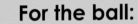
scissors

2 balloons

1

Wrap each of the cans in **colourful paper** and secure it with tape.

If the cans are empty, be careful with the sharp edges.

Cut the paper strips the same length as the can.

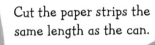

Adult ALERT!

2

To make the ball, pour a small pile of rice onto a square of clingfilm. Bring the edges together and **twist the top** of the clingfilm to keep the rice inside.

3

Carefully **cut** the **tail** off the two balloons.

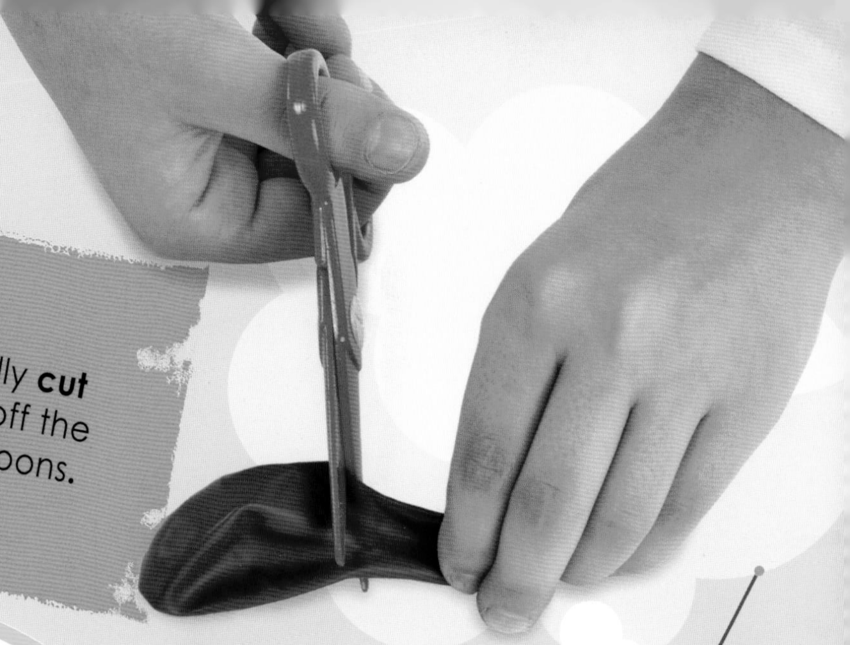

4

Stretch the first balloon to wrap it over the ball of rice. **Wrap** the second balloon to cover the hole in the first balloon.

You can also play this carnival game with a tennis ball.

Time to play!

Super subtracting

Subtracting means **taking away**. You can write how many cans you knocked down and how many are left standing as a number sentence. The **subtract sign —** means **take away**.

Count your 10 cans and stack them.

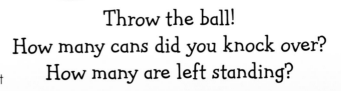

Throw the ball!
How many cans did you knock over?
How many are left standing?

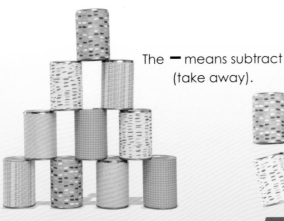

The **—** means subtract (take away).

10 - 4 = 6

This is the number you started with.

This is how many you took away.

This is the number left standing.

21

Magic pattern
wands

Make this tasty magic wand to practise repeating patterns.

Every maths wizard needs a magic maths wand! Make this tasty one with a **repeating fruit pattern**.

You will need:

strawberries

star-shaped cutter

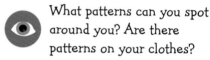

green and purple grapes

skewers

Magic maths

What patterns can you spot around you? Are there patterns on your clothes?

How does your magic fruit wand taste?

Can you clap your hands and click your fingers to make a sound pattern?

Repeating patterns

These are **a set of things** such as colours, objects, or shapes that are put in an order. Make a pattern by using the same order again and again.

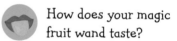

Cut a strawberry into a star shape.

The magic pattern

1 Carefully **chop the strawberries** into small bits. **Slide one piece** onto the end of a skewer.

2 Slide a **green grape** onto the skewer.

3 Slide a **purple grape** onto the skewer.

4 **Repeat the pattern**: a red strawberry bit, a green grape, then a purple grape.

5 Keep repeating the **pattern** until the skewer **is full**, then pop the strawberry star on the end.

Making patterns

This wand pattern goes red, green, purple, red, green, purple... Only the star breaks the pattern. You can make up your own pattern now. Use two different fruits for a simple pattern, or more for a **challenge**.

This pattern goes red, green, purple, red, green, purple...

23

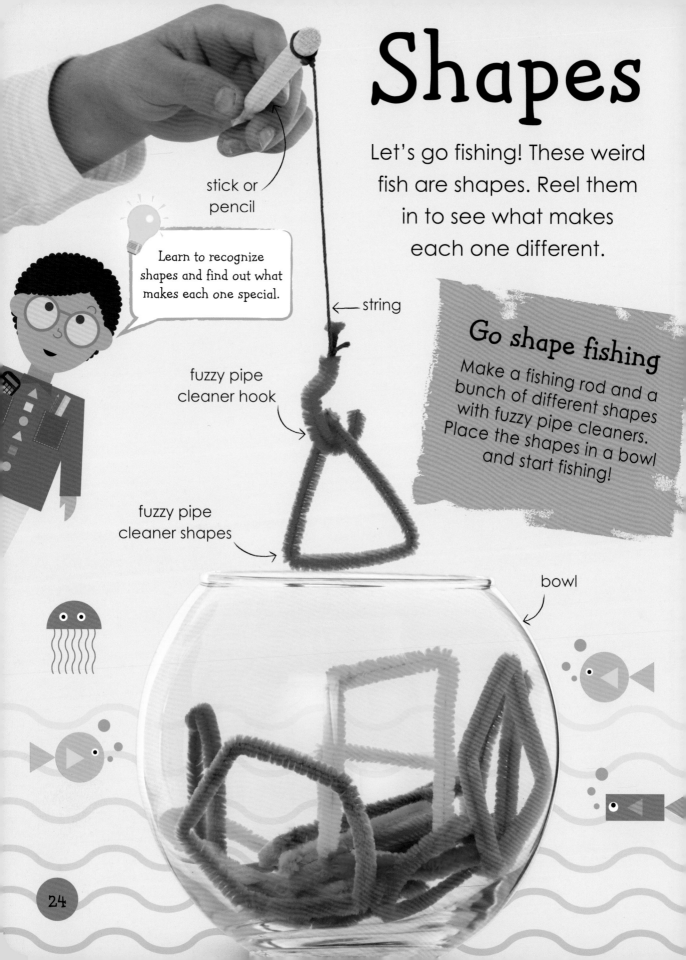

Shapes

Let's go fishing! These weird fish are shapes. Reel them in to see what makes each one different.

stick or pencil

Learn to recognize shapes and find out what makes each one special.

← string

fuzzy pipe cleaner hook

fuzzy pipe cleaner shapes

Go shape fishing

Make a fishing rod and a bunch of different shapes with fuzzy pipe cleaners. Place the shapes in a bowl and start fishing!

bowl

Get to know your shapes

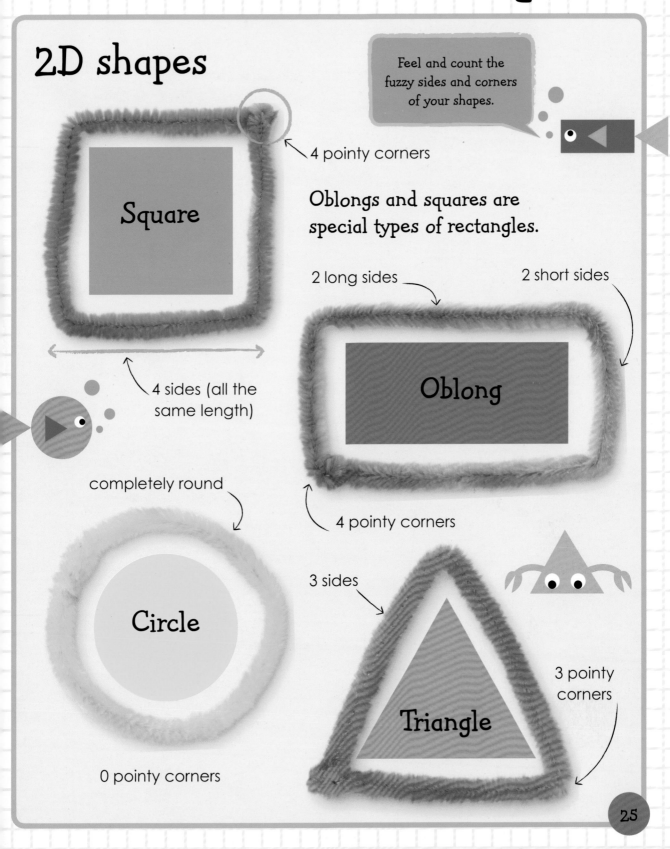

2D shapes

Feel and count the fuzzy sides and corners of your shapes.

Square

4 pointy corners

4 sides (all the same length)

Oblongs and squares are special types of rectangles.

2 long sides

2 short sides

Oblong

4 pointy corners

completely round

Circle

0 pointy corners

3 sides

Triangle

3 pointy corners

25

Make these 2D shapes
if you want a challenge!

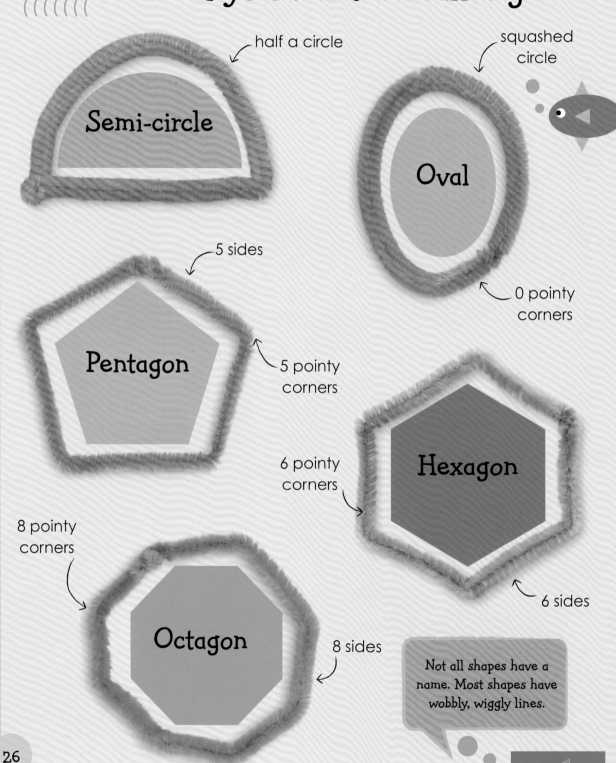

half a circle

Semi-circle

squashed circle

Oval

0 pointy corners

5 sides

Pentagon

5 pointy corners

6 pointy corners

Hexagon

6 sides

8 pointy corners

Octagon

8 sides

Not all shapes have a name. Most shapes have wobbly, wiggly lines.

3D shapes

These are 3D shapes. 3D shapes are not flat like 2D shapes. They are real, solid objects.

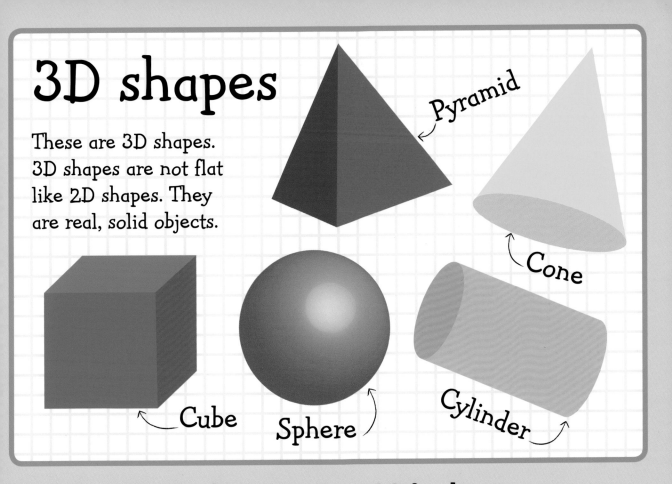

Pyramid

Cone

Cube

Sphere

Cylinder

Match each 3D shape to its real life object.

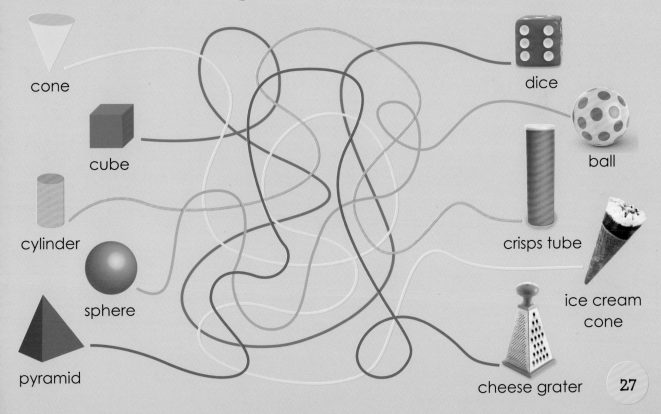

cone

cube

cylinder

sphere

pyramid

dice

ball

crisps tube

ice cream cone

cheese grater

27

Make shape aliens

Learn to recognize and name 3D shapes with this paper craft.

Make a **3D shape alien** for the planet Mathzonian. Will your alien be **long**, **round**, or **pointy?**

You will need:

paper or card

scissors

pencil

glue stick

googly eyes

1 To make a **cone alien,** copy this shape onto your paper or card. Carefully cut it out.

Adult ALERT!

The flat shape is called a net.

2 **Fold** and glue the net together to make a **cone.**

Stick on googly eyes.

Magic maths

- Can you feel and count the shapes' sides or points?

- What describing words can you think of to talk about shapes?

- Go on a shape hunt. What 3D shapes can you see around you?

3

Decorate with paper shapes to make your alien's face and arms.

Draw me a funny face!

Make alien friends!

Try making different 3D shapes so your alien has friends.

I'm a cube alien.

I'm a pointy pyramid.

Measure me

Do you know how tall you are? **Measure your height** by **comparing** it to other objects, like toys or shoes.

> Learn to measure height and length using objects as a comparison.

Make sure the chalk can wash off your floor!

1 Collect all your **shoes** together, then lie down on the floor.

2 Ask a friend to draw **a chalk line** on the floor at the top of your head and the tip of your feet.

3 **Line up** the shoes heel to toe (without gaps) between both lines.

How many shoes tall are you?

Measure your friends or your family to compare your heights. Use the same shoes to measure everyone. That way it's fair!

I'm just four shoes tall.

How tall are your toys?

You can use other things to measure yourself or your toys.

Use the same objects to measure with if you want to compare the heights of your toys.

How many cubes tall is the guitar?

How many felt-tips tall is the robot?

How many ducks tall is the recorder?

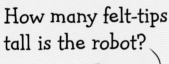

Rainbow bottles

Make this super **colourful rice** and fill jars and bottles with a rainbow, **one spoonful** at a time.

You will need:

jars and bottles of different sizes

uncooked rice

play tub or dish

food colouring

spoon

vinegar

pot with lid

1

Collect as many jars and bottles of different **shapes and sizes** as you can.

2

To make rainbow rice, put some rice, a splash of vinegar, and a few drops of food colouring into a pot.

Vinegar coats the rice *so* that the food colouring doesn't rub off.

Shake!
Shake!

3

Put the lid on your pot and **shake** it until the colour is all **mixed in**.

4

Repeat with as many colours as you like.

yellow

blue

pink

33

Pour all your colours into a play tub or dish. **Grab a spoon** and fill each jar or bottle with pretty rainbow rice. **Count each spoonful.**

Use the same spoon to fill all the jars and bottles.

Which container holds the most rice? Which holds the least?

Shake it!

Magic maths

How does your rainbow rice smell? Do you like it?

How does the sound change as you fill and shake the bottle?

Why would it be useful to know how much can fit in a bottle?

Shake the bottle as you fill it to hear how the sound changes.

nearly empty

half empty

full

Gravity scales

Learn to compare the weight of your toys with these homemade scales.

These super simple, homemade scales use gravity to **show you the weight** of your toys.

Gravity and weight

Gravity is a force that pulls everything on Earth towards the ground. Heavy things are pulled down more strongly by gravity, which is how these scales work.

When the scales are empty, they are **balanced** because the pull of gravity is the same on each side.

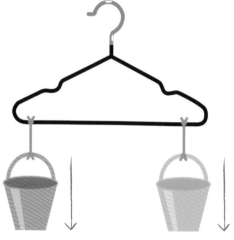

When you put toys in the pots, the pull of gravity makes the scales **tip down** on the **heaviest side**.

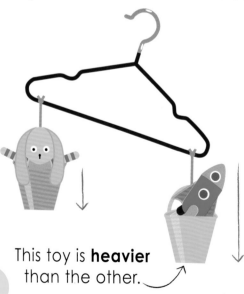

This toy is **heavier** than the other.

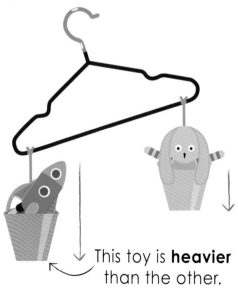

This toy is **heavier** than the other.

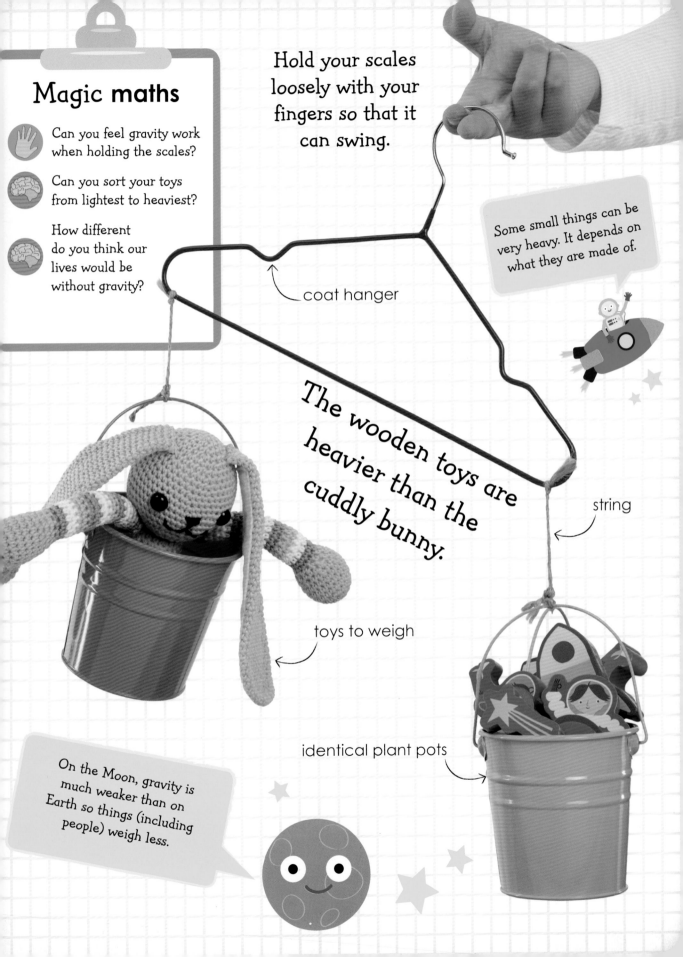

Magic **maths**

Can you feel gravity work when holding the scales?

Can you sort your toys from lightest to heaviest?

How different do you think our lives would be without gravity?

Hold your scales loosely with your fingers so that it can swing.

Some small things can be very heavy. It depends on what they are made of.

coat hanger

The wooden toys are heavier than the cuddly bunny.

string

toys to weigh

identical plant pots

On the Moon, gravity is much weaker than on Earth so things (including people) weigh less.

Wacky watches

Time isn't something you can see, but it can still be **measured**. You just need a watch or a clock.

Get crafty to learn how time is measured.

You will need:

colourful card

scissors

glue

a split pin

decorations

felt tips

tape

1 Cut out the **shapes** you need for your watch. Check the strap is long enough to go **all the way around your wrist.**

These are the shapes you need for your watch.

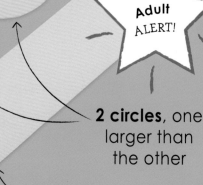

Adult ALERT!

2 arrows, one longer than the other

2 circles, one larger than the other

1 long, **rectangular** strap

2

Stick the two circles in the middle of the strap to make the **watch face**.

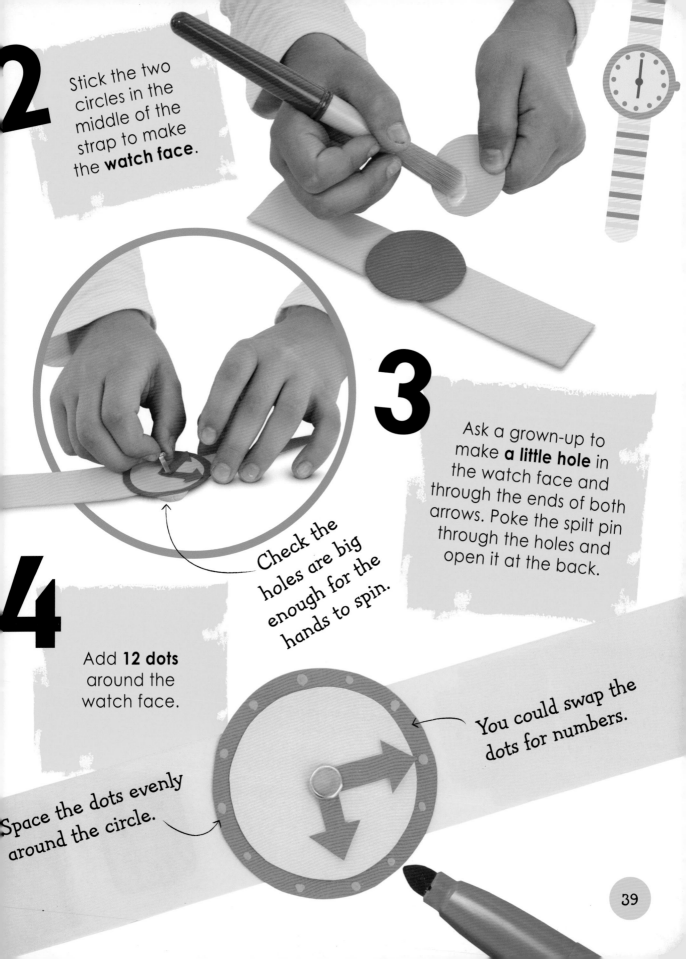

Check the holes are big enough for the hands to spin.

3

Ask a grown-up to make **a little hole** in the watch face and through the ends of both arrows. Poke the spilt pin through the holes and open it at the back.

4

Add **12 dots** around the watch face.

Space the dots evenly around the circle.

You could swap the dots for numbers.

5

Decorate your strap as you like.

How will you decorate your watch strap?

6

Put your watch on by closing the strap with tape.

Your wacky watch won't tell you the time, but it can help you practise.

Magic maths

What words can you think of that are to do with time?

Can you hear the seconds ticking on a real clock?

Do you think measuring time is useful? Why or why not?

Real watches move at the same pace to measure seconds, minutes, and hours.

I can read time!

The **little hand** tells you the **hour**. Can you see what number the little hand is pointing to?

When the big hand points **down,** that means it's **half past.**

It's 8 o'clock!

The **big hand** points to the **minutes.** When the big hand points **up,** that means it's **o'clock.**

Can you read the time on this watch?

What else can be measured?

Lots of very different things can be measured. Here are some examples:

How fast is this moving?

How much energy is in here?

How far is this?

How cold is this?

Can you think of any other things that can be measured?

41

Pizza party

Throw an easy-peasy pizza party! **Share the pizzas** with your friends and learn about **fractions** and **divisions**.

Learn about sharing things equally between different numbers of people.

You will need:

Makes 3 pizzas

3 tortilla wraps

500g (18oz) tomato sauce

500g (18oz) grated mozzarella

handful of fresh basil

On the side

12 cherry tomatoes

1 Preheat the **oven** to 220°C (425°F/Gas 7).

2 Spread a **thin layer of tomato sauce** onto each tortilla.

3 **Sprinkle** mozzarella all over the pizza.

4 Bake each pizza for 5 minutes, or **until the cheese is golden.** Top with fresh basil.

Adult ALERT!

Share your pizzas

If you divide (share) 1 whole pizza, each guest gets a fraction (an equal share) of the pizza.

If you share 1 pizza between 2 people, they each get 1 half.

Make sure your slices of pizza are all as equal as possible, so that everybody gets the same.

If you share 1 pizza between 3 people, they each get 1 third.

Add a leaf of fresh basil to each slice.

If you share 1 pizza between 4 people, they each get 1 quarter.

Magic maths

How do your ingredients smell? Do you like it?

How does your pizza taste as you eat it?

Why is it important to share things equally in maths?

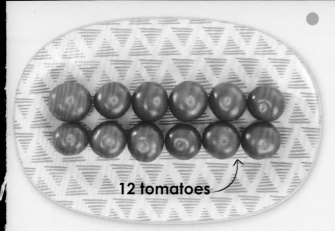

12 tomatoes

Share the side tomatoes

Divide (share) the cherry tomatoes between your friends too. Make sure everybody gets the same number so that it's fair.

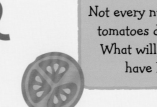

Not every number of cherry tomatoes divides equally. What will you do if you have leftovers?

If you share 12 tomatoes between 2 people, they each get 6 tomatoes.

If you share 12 tomatoes between 3 people, they each get 4 tomatoes.

If you share 12 tomatoes between 4 people, they each get 3 tomatoes.

Look, you're a maths wizard!

Now that you've played with maths, you know that maths isn't magic: it's your amazing brain working it all out! Here are maths topics to keep playing with.

Numbers

The world is full of numbers. By learning numbers and how to use them, you can count everything around you.

Keep counting until you've run out of numbers! Endless numbers is called infinity.

There's no such thing as getting things wrong in learning. Every mistake teaches you something new, so you're always learning!

Shapes

Shapes and lines are useful because they describe how things look. Some shapes have names, but most are unique and wobbly.

Patterns

Patterns can be made up of pictures, colours, numbers, or anything else that repeats itself. Being able to work out patterns is very useful. It's like guessing the future!

Create your very own pretty repeating patterns.

Measurements

From height, to time and speed, lots of things can be measured. Each measurement uses its own tool, like scales to measure weight. Measuring something just means comparing it.

Exercise your brain

With maths, you use both logic, to figure out what makes sense, and creativity, to decide how you could work it out. This brain workout can be tricky, but it's also fun.

Everyone uses maths every single day, even if they don't think about it!

Keep making maths magic!

Index